The Mind Hackers Guide to Selling

"The Science of Easily, Ethically Influencing the Human Mind"

James G Springer

"The Mind Hackers Guide to Selling"

Springer Technologies, LLC

Copyright © 2019 by James G. Springer

All rights reserved. No part of this book may be used or reproduced by any means, graphic, electronic or mechanical, including photocopying, recording, taping or by any information storage retrieval system without the written permission of the publisher except in the case of brief quotations embodied in critical articles and reviews.

Acknowledgements

My beautiful wife, who has stood by me through thick and thin, in good times and bad, for better and for worse. She's believed in me since the start and many times when I didn't believe in myself.

My parents, for always believing in me, encouraging me and never letting me give up on myself. Of all the parents in the world, if given the chance, I'd pick you. The example you set for me is a high standard that I can only hope and pray I'll someday live up to.

My good friend Troy M. Smith, who has pushed me to complete this project, whether or not I felt like it, wanted to do it or not. Troy's been an inspiration to me. I owe much of my success to this man. Our relationship, to most, would have seemed so unlikely from the beginning, but I view Troy as a brother and a co-conspirator in the quest for success.

My friend and mentor Hank Norman, for pushing me far beyond my comfort zone in so many ways to make me a better business person, speaker and writer. Hank is an inspiration and important influence on me, what I do and how I do it. He will never fully appreciate the indelible mark he has made on my life.

Table of Contents

00. Introduction — 1

01. Why Me — 7

02. The Four Primary Types of Buyer — 13

03. The Four Faces of Selling — 25

04. How and Why it Works — 31

05. The Five Keys Successful Communication — 35

06. Key #1 - Personality Profiling — 45

07. Key #2 - Body Language Analysis — 55

08. Key #3 - Deception Analysis — 65

09. Key #4 - Micro Expression Analysis — 81

10. Key #5 - Persuasion & Influence Linguistics — 85

11. Gate 3, Terminal D — 93

12. Summary — 109

« Introduction »

I believe that sales professionals are leaving millions if not tens of millions of dollars on the negotiating table every year.

I believe this is happening because they have been taught that selling is all about the mechanics, that is, about facts, functions, features, benefits and some simple psychology.

I believe that if these professionals were given the tools to complete the picture, they could massively increase their business.

I believe that any professional, sales or otherwise, who takes my training, learns the skills I teach and allows me to coach them will automatically increase their close rate / success rate by 20% or more.

How much would your life change if you were to increase your close rate by 20%? What if it were half that? Would a 10% increase do anything for you? I don't know about you, but for most of us even a 5% increase would create a staggering difference in our income.

In this book, I'm going to take you through some of the key aspects of "The Mind Hackers Guide to Selling;" how it came to be, what it does, how it works and in what way this amazingly powerful system can help you and your organization.

My goal is to leave you with actionable information that you can immediately put to use in the field. To transform your interpersonal communication skills, increase your business and enhance your personal life. And do so, in a way that's not only informative, but also enjoyable to learn.

So, let's get started.

The "Science" in "The Mind Hackers Guide to Selling" is based on aspects of advanced Neuro-Psychology and Psycho-Physiology. And though the science is advanced, "The Mind Hackers Guide to Selling" is easily learned and can be quickly implemented.

The system draws the most applicable and critical features from several modalities. They are Personality Profiling, Body Language, Deception Analysis, Micro Expression Analysis, Conversational Hypnosis and NLP. I've spent tens of thousands of dollars and as many hours learning these sciences along with over thirty years of sales training, management and executive experience.

There is no other training system in the world like "The Mind Hackers Guide to Selling." It's unique in the fact that it's completely based on scientifically proven principles of psychology, neurology and physiology. There's no fluff, no space fillers and no guesswork... only science and facts.

Additionally, most training you can get in any of the modalities I listed are taught singularly, and by a practitioner specialized in that skill set, with little practical sales, management or executive experience.

"The Mind Hackers Guide to Selling," however, is taught by a seasoned veteran from the sales and business community who is also a master practitioner and trainer in each of these modalities. That makes a big difference which sets this system even farther apart from other training programs.

Before I tell you what "The Mind Hackers Guide to Selling" is, let me stop here to tell you what it's not.

1. "The Mind Hackers Guide to Selling" is not some sort of "woo woo" program. There is no Law of Attraction, no metaphysical junk theory.

2. Everything taught is proven science

    "The Mind Hackers Guide to Selling" is not a program on the mechanics of selling. While I do offer "sales mechanics" training, I won't be teaching them in this book. You should already have a foundational knowledge of how to build your funnel, how to make cold calls, etc.

    This program dovetails perfectly into your existing sales training. It will take good training and make it exceptional and take great sales professionals into the stratosphere. So, while the training does teach how to apply these sciences to specific parts of the sales process it's not our intention to focus on the process but rather the procedure.

3. "The Mind Hackers Guide to Selling" is not only for sales professionals. This program is cross contextual.

It works equally well for executives, department heads, HR, managers, receptionists, or anyone else who interacts with others.

4. "The Mind Hackers Guide to Selling" is not a "one and done" program.

While you will be able to implement much of what I teach immediately, it will take some time and practice to get exceptional with it. Additionally, some aspects of this training you will intuitively grasp, while other parts may take some time for you to get comfortable with.

Now, with that said, I'll tell you a little about me, who I am, and why I'm qualified to teach this material.

« Chapter 1 »
Why Me?

When we see people on stage or in front of a group, we tend to freeze them in that place and time. When we see someone wearing an expensive suit, jewelry etc. or someone wearing worn clothes living on the street we intuitively believe that's who they are. It's human nature. The human mind creates a first impression of others in less than a second and locks that in. The problem is, that impression is wrong more often than it's right. Without knowing someone's story it is impossible to truly know who that person really is.

Take me for example. When you first see me, you would most likely get my story completely wrong. I was born in rural southern Indiana. When I was born my mom didn't work, as was common at that time, and my dad was making

$25/wk. on unemployment. Even in 1964 $25/wk. was no money. He got a job in a factory shortly after I was born making $75/wk. which was still no money. So, I grew up very poor.

Our home was a tiny 4 room house, which totaled about 550 sq. ft. It sat on cinder block pilings, had no running water and the bathroom was about 20 ft. or so behind the house. It was heated by a coal stove that would burn out in the night. The house would get so cold that the water bucket sitting next to it would freeze over before morning. There was nothing lavish about my life. The thing is, as a small child I didn't know we were poor. I thought everyone lived like us. To me, our life was normal.

Over the years our economic circumstances changed. By the time I graduated high school; my parents had made it into the middle class. They are now highly respected and relatively successful members of their community.

During High School and the years after, I had several jobs and got some valuable experience. I decided to start my first company at the age of 28. I had no business degree. I'd never even taken a business class and I had no real management experience. What I did have was an unjustifiable belief in myself and the product we were building.

I financed the startup with just my credit cards (Which I don't recommend by the way), and the PC I already owned. In the following three years I built that company to about $1.2 million in sales per year. I then got some really bad advice from some very good people and I lost everything I had.

Not to be deterred, I immediately started a new company as a defense contractor selling primarily to the United States Army Reserve Command (USARC). When I was 34 that company was doing about $4.5 million in sales and the profit margins were astronomical. Life was good. Until, that is, the defense budget was cut. So, faced with the choice of going back to the private sector or retiring I chose retirement.

I put all my money in the stocks of the tech companies I had dealt with for years, margined them at 45% (another thing I don't recommend) and was ready to live the good life. Not long after that the "tech bubble" burst and I lost everything again. So, I left business ownership and went back into the market place.

The following years, I spent my time building, managing and training sales teams for a variety of companies, overseeing sales well in excess of $100 million. In 2008 I experienced a major health crisis. I was diagnosed morbidly obese, Type 2 diabetic with more than four accompanying chronic illnesses. Then, in 2009 I had the misfortune of being diagnosed with a serious Mental Health issue. I was diagnosed with BiPolar1 disorder / ultra-rapid cycling with mixed episodes, which means, if I'm not on medication I experience wild polar mood swings.

Unlike a typical BiPolar1, I can have these cycles occur multiple times in a day or even an hour. I can also have a mixed episode where I experience both poles at the same time. In other words, I can be manic and depressed at the same time. This is the worst type of episode a Bi Polar can experience.

The medical bills from these two major health issues became overwhelming, and I lost everything again. While I was still managing sales teams, my health became my number one priority.

By 2010 I'd had enough of the corporate life and started a commercial painting company. Just as it was gaining traction, I was in a major car accident that left me badly injured. It took nearly two years to recover and to this day I am in pain 24/7/365.

While recovering from the illnesses I lost 145 pounds. I thought it would be great to help others lose weight, just as I had. I was wrong. In the process I discovered hypnosis. I certified as a hypnotherapist and began working on myself, as well as, transitioning the weight management company into a full-time hypnosis practice. I am very good with it, too.

I was taking so many drugs at the time I lost count. By learning to control my mind, I was able to eliminate many of the drugs, as well as, control my pain. I also helped many people learn to train their own minds to their benefit as well..

As a result of the hypnosis training and my brain injury, I became consumed with the human mind and how it works. I was already a personality profiler and went on to certify in NLP, Deception Analysis, and Micro Expression and Body Language analysis.

I became very frustrated dealing with people one on one, none of whom seemed to have any money. One day I was considering all the knowledge I had acquired, and the crazy powerful skill set I had developed. It was then I realized that this was the missing piece to all the sales training I had ever taken and given. This was the reason why sales professionals experience inconsistency in their work. It was not the message they were delivering verbally, but rather the messages they were sending and failing to recognize nonverbally.

I got excited about how all the things I'd learned applied to every business, and what it would be like for sales professionals if they understood half of what I know. It would revolutionize their business, transform their finances, and reduce the frustration of inconsistency.

So, let's move on and "take a look under the hood" of "The Mind Hackers Guide to Selling".

« Chapter 2 »
The Four Primary Types of Buyers

In your career you will meet many types of buyer classes. This is what I feel are four of the most common you will face and examples of some of the ones I've dealt with successfully. I, of course, have not been successful in many cases, but here are a few of my win's and what I learned from them.

Immediate Need Buyer –

This buyer has an immediate and desperate need for a solution. This buyer has had a major loss or failure and must get the problem resolved as quickly as possible. Price is not nearly as important as the resolution to the problem.

I had a client who called me with an emergency need for a very expensive, very uncommon hard drive for his primary server. They hadn't installed a failover server so when that single drive failed their entire network went down. I had only one supplier who had that unusually expensive drive in stock and they were in California. Distribution then was not like it is now. Even so, an overnight delivery was not acceptable to this client. He needed his network up and running. I explained the challenges to my client. He told me he didn't care what it took he needed the drive that day and left me to figure it out. The only possible solution was to have my vendor package up the drive and deliver it to the airport where I would purchase a ticket and have them check it as luggage.

The price of the ticket was not cheap, and the vendor charged extra to deliver it to the airport. I would then send someone to the airport to retrieve it and deliver it to my client. I called and told him what his cost with my markup would be and he didn't hesitate. "Get two of them," he told me. "It's costing my company thirty-thousand dollars per hour to have this network down and it's already been down for three hours." By the time I could get the drives to him, his company had lost nearly a quarter of a million dollars! Comparing the over ten-thousand dollars he paid to get the drive there and get his network up and running paled in comparison to the bloodletting that was going on without it.

This...was an immediate buyer. They are not to be taken advantage of and you should not let them take advantage of you. When you're taking extraordinary steps to take care of a desperate client you should still be paid for that effort.

Be up front about what you're doing; even ask permission if you want. The customer will remember what you saved them much more than what you charged them.

The Impending Buyer –

This buyer knows there is a problem looming on the horizon. Most of these buyers know they'll have to do something within the next three to six months. Their need is urgent but not an emergency.

> I had a prospect when I was selling engineering software and hardware that was caught with nearly one hundred copies of pirated software. At the

time that software was selling for around four-thousand dollars per seat. The manufacturer offered a reduced pricing structure and gave them a time window in order to get legal. Even though the threat to their business was eminent, they had time to get the problem resolved.

In order to sell the software, the seller has to be an authorized dealer, or at least they are supposed to be. However, there were many companies and consultants selling it who weren't. They're known in the industry as "gray marketers."

Grey marketers buy the software from an authorized reseller in another market, and then resell it at a discounted rate in order to make a 10-15% margin, and then sell their service and support to bring their margins up to around 35-50%. When we made our proposal, we went in with the manufacturers structured pricing which had a fairly thin margin, but with over one hundred copies and the required support and additional equipment. It would be the largest sale in the history of the company and at a solid margin.

The gray marketer under bid us substantially on the software but not on the high-end hardware they needed. The client told me they would purchase the equipment from us, but the gray marketer would get the software sale. The owners of the company I worked for told me there was no way they could discount the software by the amount necessary, and I would just have to give up on the sale.

Giving up is just not my style. So, I began to think of ways that we could rescue the deal. I realized that one of the higher end products we had quoted had a sale price of just over the pricing difference of the software. Then I had a revelation.

The difference in our software bid and the competitor was less than the price we'd quoted for the equipment. We would discount the sale by the price of the equipment but would only be out of pocket for the cost. It was a highly margined item too.

I offered to give the client the hardware for free if they would just pay our price for the software, which now gave us the price advantage. They went to their gray marketer who said he couldn't compete with that offer, so the prospect became a client. With the service and support I set a single sale record for the company that stood for many years and held a healthy margin on the overall sale.

This client saw a major storm on the horizon but had time to negotiate the price and assess their cost in the deal (prosecution for theft and loss of their corporate charter). Because I was creative and refused to give up, they could get the thing they had to have (the software), plus the thing they wanted to have (the equipment) for less than the competitive bid.

The Passive Buyer –

The passive buyer is one who has a non-urgent need. Generally, these clients have a six to nine-month horizon. Such as a company that replaces a fleet, computers or some other depreciating asset on a set schedule. These clients can be a solid money maker and most sellers will sacrifice margin to keep them.

When I was managing sales for a forklift dealer, one of my reps came across a potential client for a fleet of forklifts through a non-related job. We had messed that job up terribly by the way. We resolved the problem so satisfactorily that the client allowed us to bid on the replacement of their fleet. This was a division of a fortune one hundred company, so it was a big deal.

The client replaced their fleet every three years. At that facility they used them very little compared to other companies, so their fleet was nearly new even after three years. They had been buying from the same company for years and were very pleased with them. They didn't believe in service contracts, which we very much wanted to sell them. They, however, felt they were saving money by paying on individual service calls rather than paying a monthly service contract rate.

When we placed our bid, we threw everything but the kitchen sink at that deal. The president of our company was there, and the manufacturer even sent a representative to the meeting. We went all in on this bid. They thanked us, told us they were impressed, and they would let us know.

Through the debacle of the first job we did for them the sales rep and I became very close to the president of that division. She liked us and trusted us, but ultimately the decision had to be made on price. She told us we were not going to get the business, but we'd wait until the official word came down to give up.

We delivered demo units for the company to try out. They loved our product and agreed we had a far superior product, but due to their limited use, price was still king, or so they thought. We told her we would help her get her fleet in place regardless of who won the bid.

We visited that plant once every week or two for about three months through this process and I noticed a strange pattern emerging. These lifts were hardly used, yet every time we visited the competitors service tech was at the facility working on them. I asked her how much they paid for a service call.

Come to find out they were paying an industry standard hourly rate plus a trip charge every time the tech was there.

I asked her what exactly was so wrong with their fleet that it required a service person to be on-site every week. She had no answer. In fact, she didn't realize the frequency of their service visits.

She ordered an audit of their expenses. At the end of the day we replaced their fleet at our volume margin with a service agreement to cover the fleet.

It was the solid rapport and trust we built with the division president and her management team that won the deal, even when it appeared all hope was lost. We became trusted advisors willing to guide them through the purchase of a competitor's equipment. It was that trust that gave us the opportunity to demonstrate to her that the "cost" of our competitor's equipment was much higher than the "price" of ours. We converted a passive need into an immediate one.

The "It's not important" Buyer –

This buyer has a future need that is of no urgency and on no set schedule. Often these buyers are simply tire kickers. They'd like to buy sometime but it's not important right now. Unless something changes, their buy horizon is likely twelve months or longer.

I've dealt with so many of these "buyers" in the past I couldn't begin to count them. It's a judgment call as to what you want to do with this class of buyer. It's important that you not waste a lot of time chasing a "maybe" prospect, but that doesn't mean you give up on them.

When I owned my first computer company, I wanted desperately to do business with the Army Reserve base in town. They didn't have a large installation there, but that office installed, controlled and serviced all the computers in much of the southeastern United States for their division. It was a big prospect.

The problem with them was that I was a small company, growing exponentially and strapped for cash. The buyer there was a client of mine at his civilian job.

He assured me that even if he were to buy from us, we couldn't afford to carry the paper. Plus, we would need to be on the GSA contract list. I tried for nearly three years to get his business, even just a small part of it, to no avail. He didn't need me, and he had to stick to the GSA.

As my company was in its dying days before the collapse, he called me to have lunch. As fate would have it, the buying rules at the federal government had changed. He could now buy in limited amounts per transaction, off contract from local suppliers and pay with a Visa card. Unfortunately, the business wouldn't be available until too late to save my company.

I incorporated a new company for the sole purpose of retaining his corporate business and establishing myself as a defense contractor. We had built a relationship through the dealings we had in his civilian job. So, when I reincorporated, I was ready to bid. Over the next three years I did millions of dollars in business with the Reserve Command and saved them nearly as much as I charged them.

Never underestimate the power of relationship and trust. Because I had earned the buyers trust and had been willing to go the extra mile for him consistently, when the business became available it was mine, even though it took three years to get it.

Obviously, you could come up with other classes or subclasses of buyers. These four, however, encompass most of the buyers you will encounter. Regardless of the type of buyer, success with all of them depends on trust, a solid relationship and getting them emotionally invested. Getting to the point where the prospect or client is emotionally invested makes all the difference. And to the extent your prospects and clients are invested will determine failure, success and super success.

This book will demonstrate how to get your prospects and clients emotionally invested. It will show you how to communicate at a very deep level in exactly the unique way that individual naturally processes and responds to information.

« Chapter 3 »
The Four Faces of Selling

A position in Sales means different things to different people. Everyone views a career in sales a bit differently. However, there are a few primary views that define most people who enter into this amazing career.

1. **Sales as Just a Job** – To these people, sales isn't a profession, it's a job, and typically not a very fun one. Many people mistakenly believe if they can't find something better to do, they can just "do" sales. This is very prevalent in the world of retail sales, and the service industries.

   This is not totally the fault of the people who take these jobs, but rather the companies who hire them. Retail companies typically pay a minimal wage, no commissions and little reward. They hire bodies to deal with the "customers" who shop there, not to sell the company's products to actual "clients".

How much more money would retailers make if the people on their floor actually "sold" the company's products? And what if those employees believed in the company so much they actually encouraged others to shop there, rather than complaining that it's a terrible place it is to work?

2. **Sales as a Career** – The career sales person is someone who has decided to sell as a career rather than just a job. Unfortunately, most of these people are still little more than employees. They want the rewards of sales, but none of the risks.

Individuals who call themselves sales professionals but derive most or at least a large part of their income from salary are not truly sales professionals in my opinion. If their company were to kick the salary crutch out from under them most would quit instantly. This is not true in all cases but most.

Once again, this is not completely the fault of the employee. Many companies today fear sales professionals and feel the need to limit their anonymity and income. They believe that by stripping away the independence of the sales person and limiting their income, they can better control them.

Generally, these positions require the sales person to sacrifice commission in return for the safety of a salary.

What would happen if these companies shared their profits with the people who drive them? I can tell you from past experience, when there is no limit and no safety net, true sales professionals will make ridiculous amounts of money for their company and themselves.

3. **Sales as a Profession** – These are the crown jewels of sales. They are generally very independent in their work. They don't require a salary, don't care so much about the company's vacation plan, health insurance or 401k. They do, however expect (demand) to be rewarded in direct proportion to their contribution.

They provide for themselves out of the commissions they earn. They are typically very driven, focused and disciplined performers. You see these people most often in large ticket or high-volume sales companies who are forward thinking enough to allow the sales pro to make what they deserve.

How many "want to be" sales hacks would businesses weed out if this were the business model? How much money would employers save not dealing with people who are just looking for a paycheck without doing the necessary work? The company could offer a draw against commissions to provide "ramp up" time, but not as a salary. This kind of incentive fuels the sales fire. When a true professional realizes that their income is only limited by the amount of profit they can generate, and if the company's profit model is a good one, they will jump all over this type of position.

4. **Sales as a Science** – This is a different category all together. The Mind Hackers Guide to Selling can take a "Selling is Just a Job" person and turn them into sales professional and take a sales professional into a sales tactician. That is what this book is all about.

"The Mind Hackers Guide to Selling" is not about the psychology of sales. It goes far beyond mere psychology. Selling science is about neuro-psychology and psycho-physiology. It's about understanding how people think, and how to accurately predict their behavior. Since learning these skills, I am rarely surprised by anything the people I deal with do.

It's about understanding how the mind affects the body, and the body changes the mind. It's about making the stimulus / response in the sales process more predictable and thus more consistent for the sales professional.

"The Mind Hackers Guide to Selling" is not the end of the subject, but rather it's the beginning. There will be much more discovered about it in the future.

« Chapter 4 »
How and Why it Works

The power of "The Mind Hackers Guide to Selling" is in the way it works. This system is designed to take an "ALL IN" approach to interpersonal communication.

"The Mind Hackers Guide to Selling" is based on Advanced Neuro Science, Psychology and Physiology. Scientific research has learned more about the human brain in the last 50 years than in the previous 5,950 years combined. Every day we learn more and more about the amazing power of the human mind; how it works and how to manipulate/control and predict its behavioral output.

"The Mind Hackers Guide to Selling" capitalizes on this knowledge. By simply beginning to use the material here you will instantly have a huge advantage over all your competitors. You will be more relatable, sell more and close more in a way that's natural and right for you and your buyer.

The secret to "The Mind Hackers Guide to Selling" is that most of the program is designed to communicate with others in a way that goes below conscious thought. It is at this level that 97% of all decisions are made. The subconscious mind consists of the oldest and most powerful parts of the mind.

These parts of the brain are responsible for your emotions, long term memory storage, primal drives and one's criteria and values. Nothing is accepted that doesn't pass this part of the mind. If it doesn't get passed on, it doesn't get done.

Here are the 5 component parts of "The Mind Hackers Guide to Selling." They are:

1. Personality Profiling
2. Body Language
3. Deception Analysis
4. Micro Expression Analysis
5. Persuasion & Influence Linguistics

Each component contributes a unique piece of the whole and work quite nicely together. Remove just one part and the entire system loses much of its overall effectiveness. However, mastering just one of the five will still make you a more effective, more skilled communicator because they're all targeting the same part of the prospects mind.

How many times have you had a prospect completely "sold" on a proposal only to have them fail to close? Why would a person be in total agreement with all the facts and figures, features and benefits you presented, and even agree that your solution is the best but not do business with you? Reason? You "sold" them, but you didn't "persuade" them and there's a major difference.

How many times do you find yourself selling or pitching to your prospects conscious, analytical mind? And how many times do you close when the prospect has not made any emotional attachment to your product, service, or offer… almost never. What would it be like for you, if you could learn to pitch to the part of your prospects mind that actually makes the decision? That would be valuable, would it not?

These five amazingly powerful yet easily understood keys to effectively communicating will empower you to impactfully communicate with any person, anytime and anywhere. "The Mind Hackers Guide to Selling" will show you how to say what you're already saying more persuasively. It will teach you to accurately "read" how that person processes information, to see what they're feeling and to know when they are lying, all in real time. These amazing keys will help you design a new approach to interpersonal communication so that you too can reach your prospects, clients, coworkers and family in a deep and meaningful way.

Now, let's go on and look at the five keys to powerfully effective communication.

« Chapter 5 »
The Five Keys to Powerfully Effective Communication

Here we're going to go over the five key components of Powerfully Effective Communication. Each key on its own is incredibly powerful and can by itself revolutionize your business. Which means, if you were to decide that you only like number 5 but really don't like 1 – 4, or you like number 3 but not so much 1, 2, 4 &5, you'll still be infinitely more skilled at interpersonal communication than any competitor. Become proficient at them all and you'll be unstoppable.

Personality Profiling

The ability to quickly and accurately assess your prospects primary personality type gives you incredible persuasive ability.

Imagine what it would be like if you could present information in exactly the precise way in which your prospect naturally operates. How quickly do you think you could build really solid rapport? Do you think that person will be interested in listening to your presentation that's delivered in the exact way in which they naturally intake and process information? Absolutely. People like to buy from people who are like them.

"The Mind Hackers Guide to Selling" will show in great detail how to quickly and accurately elicit anyone's core personality type so you can communicate with them in a way that's most comfortable to them and where they are most easily persuaded

Body Language

This science allows you to begin to gauge the "temperature" of a prospect. As you're talking, listening or presenting to your prospect, they will transmit many more times the information nonverbally than with their words.

Suppose you could see what someone is subconsciously or consciously thinking as you are talking to or presenting to your client. You would instinctively know when your message is "landing" or when it's not. Which means, you have the opportunity in real time to adjust to meet that person's emotional requirements. How much time would you save not wasting a presentation on someone because they didn't really want to hear what you were saying? And, how much money would you save or make, having the ability to recognize true interest or disinterest in real time?

"The Mind Hackers Guide to Selling" will show you how to spot the subtle subconscious body movements of the people you're meeting every day, which means you're in control of any and every interaction.

Deception Analysis

We all lie. And, we're not very good at it. Lies leave clues if you know what to look for. The truth is, the average person, regardless of their job training does a very poor job detecting lies. On average a person who is not trained specifically in deception analysis, when looking for lies, will catch only about 54% of the lies they're told. When not focusing on catching lies, 80% of the lies that are told will slip by unnoticed. That's a lot of lies missed, when you consider that we are lied to between twenty and two hundred times per day. What's important however, is not "Whether" someone lies, but rather "Why" they lie. For what purpose did the person tell you the lie?

How many times has a client, prospect or co-worker lied to you, only for you to find out too late that you had been duped? How much money have you lost because a prospect strung you along telling they were going to buy, only to find out later, they never had any intention to buy from you? I know, in my career, missing lies has cost me a small fortune. Not only in trying to do business with the liar, but also in the lost business I could have gotten from a legitimate buyer.

"The Mind Hackers Guide to Selling" teaches you how to quickly and easily spot liars in your presentations, negotiations and day to day conversations. If you want to powerfully enhance your ability to communicate, deception analysis key.

Micro Expression

This science takes body language and deception analysis to a whole new level. Micro Expressions are emotional "leaks" that present themselves as a full or partial facial expression lasting from $1/5^{th}$ to $1/2$ second in duration. The real beauty in the ability to accurately see micro expressions is they are subconscious and cannot be controlled. Just having the ability to see someone's true emotion at a given time will give you instantaneous feedback as to what that person is truly feeling. Many times, the person doesn't even know they are experiencing the emotion.

These flashes of true emotion allow the practitioner to not only gauge the honesty of a person but will also allow you to see if a prospect is suppressing their true feelings. They may be trying to hide their happiness about your proposal, or maybe hide their fear about your price. If you cannot see these very subtle emotional leaks, you're missing business and missing profit.

How many times have you discovered that you left money on the negotiating table after you'd already closed? And how many times did you think your proposal was going great, when in fact you completely turned them off. Think about how much better your business would be if you could quickly and accurately see what a person is feeling.

"The Mind Hackers Guide to Selling" will show you how to accurately recognize these emotional leaks, which means you can quickly and instinctively tailor your presentation in real time in order to find the underlying source of these hidden or suppressed emotions.

Persuasion and Influence Linguistics

Even though body language experts often talk about the minimal contribution our words have in face to face conversation, it doesn't have to be that way. In reality, our words often drive much of nonverbal communication. Using language properly is not only knowing about what you say, but in what way you say. This is key to effectively communicating with someone else at a very deep level. We ask good questions but ask them the wrong way.

We often believe that we sell on logic, but that's not true. The majority of decisions we make, regardless of price or importance, are made in the lower regions of the mind. In order to persuade another person, you must first know how to communicate at that emotional level, to get the prospect, "in their head," so to speak.

"The Mind Hackers Guide to Selling" will show you in what way you should restructure what you're already saying. Or, help you design a new approach to interpersonal communication. Doing so allows you to reach your prospects, clients, coworkers and even family in a deep and meaningful way. In order to get maximum results from your verbal communication, proper use of language is vital.

Now we'll take a closer and deeper look at each of the 5 keys to powerfully effective communication.

« Chapter 6 »
Personality Profiling

The first key in powerfully effective communication is personality profiling. You have most likely heard of personality profiling in the past. Generally, one would take a test of up to twenty pages. The test would then be scored, and the results of the findings would be returned in a large report. The report defines your individual "temperament" / "communication style"... your personality. There are literally dozens of personality profiling systems. However, most, when boiled down, break into four general character traits. Introvert vs Extravert and People vs Task orientation.

The system I use is called the DISC profile. With DISC a person's primary personality falls into one of four overall categories.

- Extraverted / Task oriented, the "D" personality
- Extraverted / People oriented, the "I" personality
- Introverted / People oriented, the "S" personality
- Introverted / Task oriented, the "C" personality.

And while "The Mind Hackers Guide to Selling" teaches a quick and easy way to assess someone's core personality, my coaching clients will at some point be required to take the full assessment and receive the fifty-page report. This report gives insight not only to that person's individual personality mix, but also shows how to work with other personality types. It suggests what positions best suit their personality. It also shows what they naturally like and dislike when it comes to interaction and information, and the group dynamics of the total team.

Our personalities don't fit completely into one of the four-character designations. We all have some degree of each, but there typically will be only one primary. Also, personalities are contextual. A person may be a "High D" at work, a "High C" at home, and a "High I" socially. Some people shift based on context some don't. I, for example, am a "High D" personality at work, at home and socially. I have, however, through a great deal of work learned to "raise" the most beneficial category in context. When I work with someone they almost always believe my personality is the same as theirs.

The DISC system will show one's personality in totality including contextual change information. The beauty of the DISC system is that it also allows for a quick generalized assessment of a person's contextual personality.

If you're watching, and listening, you can see the signs of introversion and extraversion. You can also hear signs of whether a person is more people or task orientated. At that point you will have a pretty accurate assessment of that person's personality.

Note that personality profiling is not a one and done exercise, people's personality's change. A person can be a strong "D" personality at one meeting then become a strong "C" in another. This is why you should always be checking. Never go into a meeting assuming the person will be the same as they were in the last meeting.

Here's some specific information on each and the way each personality thinks.

The High "D" personality –

High "D's" are typically highly productive, driving, demanding doers.

- They need to be right
- They like to be in control
- They don't like details
- They don't like wasting time
- They make decisions quickly, often on gut instinct
- They change their minds very slowly
- They don't like weak people
- They enjoy conflict and debate

When dealing with a high "D" you want to keep your presentation very tight. Give them top and bottom line information. If there's a detail they think is important they'll let you know. Be strong and confident, but let them think they are in control, even when they're not. Pie charts, graphs and spreadsheets are typically not liked by the high "D."

Stay out of the tall grass when dealing with them. Know your stuff. Be prepared. Even if they don't really care about a detail, they may well ask you just to see if you know what you're doing.

The High "I" personality –

The high "I" is commonly the person who craves attention. They like to be involved in everything.

High "I's" are very inspirational, interesting, impulsive people.

- They need excitement
- They love to have fun
- They are great starters'
- They are lousy finishers
- They crave the spotlight
- They make decisions very quickly based on how they "feel"
- They change their mind as quickly as they make it.
- They have little use for details, as details are boring

When dealing with a high "I," keep your presentation light, interesting and brief. "I's" have very short attention spans. If possible, get them engaged in the presentation. Ask them questions; have them do things as the presentation proceeds. Stay away from too much details. "I's", like "D's" are extraverted but in a different way. An "I" would say, "<u>I</u> need to be in the front of the room.", while a "D" would say, "<u>They</u> need me in the front of the room."

Be prepared to keep your presentation on track. "I's" are easily distracted and like to chase things down the rabbit hole and will try to take you with them. Stay on your toes. "I's" will also try to trip you up, just because it's fun to do.

The High "S" personality –

The high "S" will often be found in support roles because that's their nature. They make an excellent follower, which doesn't mean you won't see them in leadership. An Executive VP is a leader to most but is still a support person to the President and CEO.

The "S's" are typically the supportive, soft spoken, stable people in an organization.

- They don't like to be the center of attention, in fact, they hate it.
- They are great hard-working employees
- They don't like conflict or drama
- They make decisions very slowly (if at all)
- They change their mind quickly in order to get along with others.

When meeting with a high "S," speak slowly and a little more softly. Emphasize team play, support and other words that show caring and meaning. Use a lot of emotional words, but not drama or conflict words. "S's" will reject anything that involves controversy or conflict. Show them how what you're doing will mitigate conflict and drama and you will instantly have their attention.

The High "C" personality –

You will often see the high "C" in technical analytical roles in an organization. They love to sift through details and micromanage.

The high "C" is generally a cautious, careful, consistent person. They're introverted so they may come off as somewhat aloof or standoffish.

- They need a lot of data
- They don't mind conflict
- They need more information. They love pie charts, pivot tables, charts, graphs, etc.
- They make decisions very slowly
- They change their mind as slowly as they make it
- They like details more than just top and bottom lines as the "D's" do
- They are extremely methodical and deliberate in their thought process

For many sales pro's this is the person they most like dealing with because they are all about the logic and rationality of the project. However, since everyone is assuming the "C" type makes their decision on logic they are incorrect. "C's", like everyone else, make 97% of their decisions based on emotion which makes the hardest to persuade. When you meet with a "C" make sure you know your stuff. These people thrive on minutia and they expect others to do the same.

So, that's a short description of the four primary personality types. And, I'm sure you can see the value in understanding the way your prospects, clients, coworkers and even family process information. This is the first key to effectively powerful communication skills. The more you understand about the power of personality profiling the more you will see your communication skills increase, which means, you will close more deals and create positive, productive relationships.

« Chapter 7 »
Body Language Analysis

The second key in powerfully effective communication is Body Language or Nonverbal Communication. Recognizing, interpreting and responding to the nonverbal communication of others, while communicating the desired nonverbal message is the second key to powerfully effective communication.

The term "body language" doesn't actually describe the science properly. "Body Language" implies that it deals only with the movements of the physical body. It should actually be referred to as "nonverbal communication." Nonverbal communication is, as it implies, any communication that does not directly use words.

There is nonverbal physical and nonverbal voice. A frown is an example of physical nonverbal communication. If I'm frowning, you don't need me to tell you anything to know I'm unhappy. What you do with that signal is critical to success.

If I make a statement but my command tone goes up at the end, I'm asking a question. If I ask a question but my command tone goes down at the end, I'm making a statement or issuing a command. In these examples you can see that the words don't express the true meaning, it is the voice.

One of the reasons why a sales professional may get mixed results from an identical presentation is nonverbal communication. If their body and tonality are incongruent with their spoken message, they will most likely fail to effectively communicate the message in the way they intended.

Nonverbal communication is very primitive. It predates spoken language. To this day there are cultures where spoken language is nearly nonexistent, yet they can communicate very effectively. Nonverbal communication is incredibly powerful, yet most don't know how to read it consciously. However, we do read it subconsciously.

If you've ever watched a presentation where you agreed with the words, but something about the presentation just didn't "feel right", you've likely had a subconscious encounter with nonverbal communication.

When our verbal message is incongruent with our nonverbal message, even an untrained person will intuitively know. It's part of our primitive programming as humans. They just don't know how to reconcile the verbal message they are hearing with the nonverbal messages they're receiving unconsciously.

We convey massive amounts of information through nonverbal voice communication. We use our pitch, pace, tone, timber, volume, command tone and inflection to name a few. These all involve the voice but are not revealed directly as words.

Take for example the following sentence; "I didn't take your pencil." With no inflection or command tone change it's just a statement of fact. If, however, you begin emphasizing one specific word in the statement you radically change its meaning.

"**I** didn't take your pencil." (It wasn't me)

"I **didn't** take your pencil." (I thought about it but didn't)

"I didn't **take** your pencil." (I just borrowed it)

"I didn't take **your** pencil." (I took someone else's)

"I didn't take your **pencil**." (I took your pen)

You can see from this simple exercise how simply changing the inflection on one word completely changes the message the sentence is meant to convey.

Our bodies convey even more data than our nonverbal voice. From macro and micro expressions of the face to the movements of our hands and feet, the body is in constant communication. Even when someone doesn't move at all it's still conveying a message.

I've seen meme's on social media with a list of items that take "no skill" to do, and one of the items is always "Body Language." This meme annoys me, because effectively reading and displaying body language is absolutely a skill. It takes a lot of work in order to learn how to accurately read the body language of someone. It takes even more skill to make sure your body language is conveying the right or congruent message.

Gesticulation is one of the more common aspects of nonverbal communication. The way we gesture during a presentation can make or break it, to the extent that it costs you the business. Natural gestures flow smoothly through the subconscious and out through the body. Therefore, it's a good idea to film your presentation a few times prior to delivery then watch the video focusing on what you see and hear from a nonverbal perspective.

You may be surprised by how many of your gestures look forced, unnatural, incongruent, etc. By practicing your nonverbal communication, you can adjust it and watch again. You continue this process until the proper gestures become natural, smooth and subconscious. At that point you can be confident that your nonverbal communication will enhance your message rather than to distract or detract from your message.

Here's a quick look at three of the most common gestural types you'll see in a presentation. I call them body language "PIE." Of all the gestures we make, most will fall into one of these three categories.

P – Pacifiers

I – Illustrators

E – Emblems

Pacifying Gestures are just as you would expect. They are movements we make to try and soothe ourselves. If you think back to your childhood, you'll see the basis of these deadly presentation gestures. You want to avoid these gestures at all costs in your presentations, whether you're presenting to a group, or an individual, pacifying gestures are to an audience as blood in the water is to a shark. They are demonstrations of anxiety, fear and lack of confidence.

These gestures include but are in no way limited to:

- Touching the face

- Rubbing the hair

- Stroking the back of the hand or arm

- Rubbing or wringing hands

- Picking imaginary fluff

- Adjusting collar, cuffs, sleeves or any other clothing

- Rubbing the back of the neck

There are a host of other indications of stress. Avoid these gestures at all costs unless demonstrating stress or anxiety in a story, which makes it illustrative not pacifying.

Illustrative Gestures are nonverbal punctuation in a presentation. They add power and punch to your delivery when done naturally. They can also be used to illustrate something we're describing, such as moving the hands in a circle while describing a ball.

Some Illustrative gestures you'll see are:

- Power "pointing"

- The hand chop

- Holding the ball

- Palms up / Palms down

- Finger snap

- Steepled Hands

There are many more of these energy enhancing and diminishing gestures. Use Illustrators as much as possible without it seeming forced. This is something that's ideally rehearsed so they become natural and can be implemented with appropriate timing.

Emblematic Gestures are body movements that need no words to describe what they mean. Just as you know the meaning of a red octagonal sign, emblematic gestures need no description.

All emblematic gestures are not universal. Some have vastly different meaning in other cultures. So, make sure you know the cultural emblematic gestures for where ever you are outside the U.S.

Examples of Emblematic Gestures would be:

- Thumbs up / Thumbs down

- The peace sign

- The middle finger

- Shaking / nodding the head

- Palm out – Stop

There are many, many more of these incredibly powerful gestures. Emblems add visualization to a presentation and since the vast majority of people are visual, adding these gestures to your presentation engages the subconscious mind of your audience very effectively.

This has been a very, very basic view of the second key to powerfully effective communication. Understanding nonverbal communication is critical as it's the driving force behind many of the other keys.

Let's move on now to the third key to powerfully effective communication: Deception Detection and Analysis.

« Chapter 8 »
Deception Analysis

The third key in powerfully effective communication is learning to know when someone is lying. Whenever I speak, Deception Analysis, or Human Lie Detection, is always an audience favorite.

Most people don't think about the staggering amount of deception we are exposed to and perpetrate on others. When speaking, I always ask the question, "How many here are liars?" there are always some who are honest and admit they lie, but most typically don't.

As I said earlier, we all lie, we do it a lot, and we're very bad at it. In fact, on average we will lie 2.94 times per 10 minutes of conversation. This is especially true when speaking to a stranger.

Also, every business transaction includes deception. It is important to remember, anything that is not 100% true is 100% a lie. The number one lie we tell is, "I'm fine."

No matter your social status, religious affiliation, race or creed, we all lie. The important aspect of being able to detect deception is not catching a lie, it's uncovering the truth. If for example at the conclusion of a presentation the prospect says, "Everything sounds good," while simultaneously shaking their head "no," there's a 99.997% probability that person is lying to you. And, they're not even conscious of what their body is doing to betray them.

Much of what is included in the "Body Language" section of this book dovetails into deception analysis. Earlier, I mentioned congruence between what the body says vs what the words say. When our words and movements are in contrast with each other, as with the previous example, it is a fair bet the person is not being completely honest.

Our words also betray us when we lie. The difference between the way a person speaks when telling the truth vs when they are telling a lie is noticeable if you know what to look for.

We lie in a variety of ways for many reasons. Sometimes we don't consider lying to be necessarily deceptive or bad. However, lying rarely leads to a positive outcome. Lying, though we all do it, is not something that the subconscious mind is capable of, therefore it always tells the truth. This is how deception experts are able to determine whether or not a person is lying.

The four primary reasons we lie are to

- protect others from harm

- to protect our self from harm

- make someone else look better

- make our self look better

There are many categories or types of lies we tell. They vary in "value," or consequences. The "value" of the lie will determine the degree to which they may be detected. A very low value lie will generally produce very minimal indication of deception. A high value lie will typically produce more noticeable deception indicators.

Here are a few of the many types of lies we tell.

White Lies – This type of lie is one that is rarely malicious. We use this lie many times to protect the feelings of others. If a person loves an outfit, a new car, etc. and you feel it is ugly, unflattering, a bad decision or whatever, you may be inclined to tell a white lie to protect their feelings and claim to like or approve of whatever it is. However, your lie could ultimately hurt that person anyway.

When someone trusts you enough to ask your opinion, they generally want your honest opinion. You don't need to be cruel or unfeeling, but you can tactfully and empathetically tell someone your true feelings. If someone asks what you think about something and you lie, thinking you're protecting them you may be doing the exact opposite.

Lies of Omission – Many times we tell this type of lie to protect our self. In a lie of omission, we don't directly lie to someone, we simply leave out details that may be painful to tell. This is a very common way of lying. It may be very difficult for someone who is not trained in deception analysis to detect, because a lie of omission typically contains some truth. For example, if someone is telling a chronology, they can tell the truth throughout the story but conveniently leave something out and simply "jump over" the part of the chronology they don't want you to know.

Lies of omission may be of either high or low value. If your spouse asks you what took you so long getting home and you give her the chronology of your trip, buy conveniently leave out the fact that you stopped at the gas station to buy a lottery ticket, that would be deceptive as a lie of omission, but unless you're a gambling addict it is probably not a high value lie. If, however, you left out the fact that you stopped on the way home to see your lover, that would be of much higher value.

Lies of Exaggeration – We commonly see this lie where a person wants to make their self appear better than they are, or where someone wants to make someone else appear better or even worse than they are. This type of lie is very commonly seen in interviews, résumés, sales presentations and online dating profiles. Depending on where you are in the world on average as many as 60% of people lie on their résumé and around 90% lie on dating profiles. Lies of exaggeration can also be low or high value lies depending on the context of the lie.

If in an interview, a sales person says they averaged 123 outbound calls per day at their last job, and really averaged around 50, it's a lie, but may have little negative impact so long as the person, if hired, meets the requirements of that job. If, however, in the same interview the sales person says they have 10 years' experience managing large sales teams and in fact have two years' experience managing very small teams, it could be a major problem were that person to be hired.

Lies of Direct Deception – These are most commonly high value lies where the liar is trying to avoid the consequences of their behavior. They may sometimes occur when trying to keep someone else from suffering the consequences of theirs, as well. These lies can include lies of omission or lies of exaggeration but can include others as well. When directly or maliciously lying the person may fabricate an entire narrative that is untrue. They may look you straight in the eye and simply lie to you. Most people think a liar will avoid eye contact. That's not true. When a person is being directly deceptive, especially when the stakes are high, they will often lock eyes with the person to whom they are lying. They need to make sure the other person is "buying the lie". Plus, they think it makes them appear more honest.

This type of lie will typically cause more deception indicators to appear. Lying is very difficult and tends to cause "cognitive overload" and enter a state of "Fight/Flight," simply because of the many things the liar must do simultaneously. Also, the mere consequences of being caught can cause a person to become cognitively overloaded. When a person enters the state of "Fight/Flight," their entire nervous system changes, causing the person to move or speak (deception indicators) in ways that a trained deception expert will notice, but an untrained person will miss. These indicators typically go mostly unnoticed by the liar, as well, because they occur at an unconscious level.

Psychopathic & Sociopathic Lies – Psychopathy and Sociopathy are categories all to themselves. These are forms of mental illness in which the person's lack of empathy and their twisted sense of emotion make their deception nearly impossible to detect unless specifically trained in that area. For that reason, I'm not going to cover these here, other than to mention they exist and they don't lie as a normal person does.

There are over one hundred deception indicators I teach in this program. The system is uncommon in that deception indicators are weighted based on how many times in the study of over one thousand high value interrogations each indicator was seen on its own and the person was later proven to have lied.

I'm going to give you a few very common and, some of the most accurate deception indicators both physical and verbal. Keep in mind that no deception indicator is 100% accurate on its own. We also don't typically have the luxury of sitting down and interrogating someone we may think is lying, establishing a baseline and watch for lies.

Baselining – Ideally, we'd be in an interview situation where we can get a very accurate baseline of a person's behavior both honest and dishonest. It's more difficult in a conversation, but you can still learn much about the person's normal behavior and what you can or cannot use as a deception indicator.

If, for example, the person has allergies and is constantly scratching or touching their nose, you can't accurately use that indicator.

We must rely on probabilities and "clusters" in order to know for certain that someone is lying. All the indicators

I'm sharing here have a 90% or higher probability of indicating deception without any other deception indicator. So, any of the following indicators when coupled with even a low probability indicator such as "pointing a foot toward an exit," at 10%, is enough to determine that a person is in fact lying.

Keep in mind these are only deception indicators in response to a relevant threatening question where lying will have undesirable consequences.

Verbal Deception Indicators

Removal of contractions –

Everyone naturally uses contractions in their normal speech. However, when in response to a relevant threatening question a person suddenly drops all the contractions and starts using emphatic language, there is a 90% probability that person is lying to you. For example, in response to the question, "Why did you contact my prospect?" the normal response would be "I didn't contact your prospect." A dishonest response would be, "I did not contact your prospect."

Keep in mind that some very technical people or academics naturally use emphatic language so this indicator would not apply to them.

Removal of personal pronouns –

We normally speak using personal pronouns. I, I'm, she, her, him, his, etc. are all common in speech. If a person suddenly changes to distancing language you will hear things such as: that woman, the gentleman etc. This is the person's conscious mind messing up their language. It sounds completely normal to them but if you pay attention you'll notice.

For example, the honest response to the question, "Did you quote Dave's client?" would be "No, I didn't quote his client." The dishonest response may be, "I didn't quote the guy's client." It sounds natural to the liar, but you can see, it is very unusual.

Indirect answer to a direct question –

This is a very common deception leak. Once you know about it, you'll see it all the time. When you ask someone a direct relevant threatening question and the person does not answer directly, they are most likely lying.

If for example I were to ask someone, "did you take my pen?" and the person responds with, "I'm an honest person, I don't need your pen." This is a simple yes/no question and doesn't need a long answer. This person is most likely lying because they didn't actually answer your question. It was a simple yes/no question.

Convincing language –

Another common form of deception is using convincing language in response to a relevant threatening question. Convincers are designed to try to make the other person believe their lie.

When someone responds with; "Swear to God," "I'm only going to say this once," "Honestly," "To tell you the truth," and many others, they are trying to convince you they're telling the truth.

For example, a person is asked, "Why were you late to work?" an honest response might be, "I got stuck in traffic on the interstate." A dishonest statement may be, "Honestly, I got stuck in traffic."

Physical Deception Indicators

Inconsistent head nodding – This is an example of the subconscious answering with the truth while the person is lying with their words. It is an emblematic gesture done subconsciously, so the speaker has no idea they've done it. You will see a person, sometimes very slightly, shake their head "no" while saying "yes" or nodding "yes" while saying "no."

The one-sided shrug – Most gestures are symmetrical but when lying the person will often times show only one side of the gesture. If you watch an interview where the person being interviewed is "cornered" by the interviewer, you will very often see this gestural slip.

While telling the lie one of the liar's shoulders will come up slightly, as if to say, "I have no confidence in what I just said." This indicator is not limited to a shoulder. The person can also shrug a hand. The meaning is the same. Watch and you'll see it quite commonly.

A gesture out of sync with statement – When we gesture naturally, our gestures are in sync with what we're saying. They will present slightly before or during the statement. When a person is in cognitive overload due to telling a relevant lie, they will sometimes try to force a gesture.

Unfortunately, for the liar the subconscious mind is about 1 ½ times faster than the conscious mind and the movements will get out of sync. One gestural failure you commonly see is the hand chop. When telling the truth while making a point the hand will chop at slightly before or during the point being made. When lying, the gesture gets all over the place timing wise.

Touching the face – A very common and tell-tale sign of deception is touching the face in response to a threatening relevant question, especially the nose. If someone answers a threatening question and immediately touches their nose or face, they're most likely lying.

Putting it all together – A wife asks her husband, "Who is she?" and the husband replies, "Honestly, I don't know the woman." while nodding slightly. In this example, the husband used a convincer (honestly), ended the statement with distancing language (the woman), then capped it off with an incorrect emblematic gesture (nodding slightly). He's lying, there is no doubt.

So, that was six of the most common deception indicators you will see and hear. Remember the purpose is not catching a lie, it's finding the truth. It may sound easy and pretty straight forward when reading it like this, but conversation moves very quickly, so the lies are easily missed.

Even someone who is completely trained and practiced in deception analysis will still struggle to get over 80-85% accurate and rarely over 90%, which is, actually pretty amazing. When you consider that a person who is not trained specifically in deception analysis when looking for a lie, is only 54% accurate. And, when not specifically looking for deception will miss about 80% of the twenty to two hundred lies they're told daily.

Now we'll go to the fourth key in powerfully effective communication. This key will take your emotional intelligence, body language and deception analysis skills to a level you wouldn't have thought possible. That key is, micro expressions.

« Chapter 9 »
Micro Expression Analysis

The fourth key to powerfully effective communications is the ability to accurately see and interpret micro expressions. This ability is without a doubt one of the most powerful communication skills one can learn from "The Mind Hackers Guide to Selling".

A micro expression is a full or partial expression that lasts approximately 1/5th to 1/2 a second. In order to see them consistently and accurately takes considerable training and extensive practice. However, once you've learned the skill, micro expression recognition cannot be "turned off".

Also used in deception analysis, micro expressions are a subconscious leak of true emotion. When being deceptive, this leakage occurs because a person's emotions are in contrast with what they're saying, hearing or experiencing.

The subconscious mind has no capacity for lying. It always tells the truth. Therefore, the true emotion a person feels will always leak out. The person is also not conscious of the leak. Two exceptions would be:

1. A rehearsed speech practiced to the point that the emotions are removed.

2. When the person is a psychopath or sociopath

Though we like to think our emotions are complicated they can be distilled down to a few basic emotions. It's important to note that emotions are universal and not cultural as are emblematic gestures. Emotions are displayed the same in every culture around the world.

There are seven basic emotions:

1. Happiness

2. Sadness

3. Anger

4. Surprise

5. Fear

6. Contempt

7. Disgust

In addition, a person can show a neutral expression which makes up the eight primary facial expressions. Keep in mind there can be thousands of different muscular combinations, but these are the primary emotions that drive the expressions.

Most people have a difficult time in recognizing them all because some are so similar, and they never consciously considered what the face is doing when expressing an emotion, be it genuine or fake.

For example. In surprise, fear and sadness, the eye brows all move similarly but once trained, you'll see there are major differences in the muscle groups used to make the expressions.

Happiness and contempt are also very similar but use different muscle combinations and flexion. Contempt is the only asymmetrical expression. In contempt the lip corner is slightly higher on one side.

You will also commonly see a person "masking" in an attempt to hide their true emotions. The most common is a masking smile. Unfortunately for the person masking, if you learn this skill, you'll still see the underlying emotion.

You will often see someone display a "fake" smile while trying to cover any of the other emotions. A contempt smile, for example be very difficult to see because both corners of the lips turn up. However, one side will be only slightly higher than the other.

You will also see other combinations of expressions, or rapid successions of emotions. It is very common to see a person who has "mixed emotions" about something. You may see a flash of happiness immediately followed by contempt, or anger mixed with disgust. There are literally thousands of possible combinations. Some that even signal a potential physical or emotional assault.

As I stated earlier, micro expression recognition comes only with a great deal of instruction and even more practice. I've watched thousands of practice videos to get to my level of proficiency.

Now we move on to the fifth and final key to powerfully effective communication and the only one that is not nonverbal, Persuasion and Influence language.

« Chapter 10 »
Persuasion & Influence Linguistics

The fifth and final key to powerfully effective communication is persuasion and influence language. This is the only verbal key in "The Mind Hackers Guide to Selling" and is tremendously important. The spoken word typically doesn't transmit as much information as does nonverbal communication but that doesn't mean it's not powerful or that it should be ignored. In fact, our words are often the driving force behind the other four keys.

What you say is not nearly as important as how you say it. I'm not talking about voice control, grammar or syntactic proficiency but rather word and phrase control. This key is all about structuring your verbal communication in a way that reaches below the consciousness of the other person.

As you become more and more proficient at doing this, you'll notice that you're much more persuasive, more charismatic and more interesting to talk to. You could even get to the point where people want to talk to you simply because they feel good when they do. The key to all this is speech patterns made up of what renowned Conversational Hypnotist, Igor Ledochowski, calls "Power Words" and "Power Phrases."

Considering the limited space of this book, I will be able to only scratch the surface of this vast and important skill.

We all used patterned language of some sort. The problem is, we've become very lazy with our language and with the advent of social media, we are declining more and more rapidly.

The language patterns taught in "The Mind Hackers Guide to Selling" are specifically designed to bypass critical thought and directly impact the unconscious processes in the minds of those with whom we communicate. Additionally, these words and phrases can not only be used in spoken communication, but in written text, email and even on social media.

I will give you a few to consider adding to your daily vocabulary and the context of your communication.

The first are called presuppositions. Presuppositions are language patterns where we "Presuppose" something as a suggestion or command.

For example, there is the:

- Adverb / Adjective
- Complex Equivalent – a=b
- Cause and Effect – a causes b
- Temporal
- Ordinal
- Spatial

and many more.

I don't have time here to dissect these and do them one at a time, but if you were to put them together it might look something like this:

"As you begin to utilize these amazingly powerful language patterns, you'll notice that you are quickly becoming a more interesting, and impactful communicator. Which means, the more you use these language patterns the more you'll find yourself instinctively, intuitively using them in your daily conversations in a way that attracts people to actually want to speak to you."

Now, you may not want to use these patterns in a blitz like I just did, though sometimes you might. The key is being aware of them and using them as much as possible. It may seem that you sound strange at first, but once proficient it sounds completely normal.

Doing simple things such as placing your adverbs and adjectives before the noun or verb they're modifying, or starting more sentences with, "as you begin," or "Find yourself," "the more _____the more____" completely changes the dynamic of your speech and allows your message to smoothly flow from you, directly into the subconscious mind of the other person(s) with whom you communicate.

Then there are linguistic "Power Words" and "Phrases" taught in the training. Some examples, and they may not make total sense outside the training, would be:

- Imagine
- Suppose
- What would it be like
- It's as if
- I can't tell you
- You really should

- Tag Questions: shouldn't you, couldn't you, should you not, can't you, etc.

These are only a few examples. I teach many more.

An example would be: "Imagine what it would be like for you if you could speak to others at a level below consciousness. And suppose you became very proficient using these power words in your daily communication. It's as if you were creatively and effectively communicating directly with the subconscious mind of your listener. Now, I can't tell you if you'll be able to do this sooner or maybe a little later. And you really should know that using these power words and phrases is easy to learn and understand once you've practiced them to the extent that they've simply become a part of the way you naturally speak. Is it not?"

Once again, this is a kind of linguistic blitz that you would rarely do, unless you really wanted to change your voice pitch, slow your pace and just zap someone's brain with it.

Becoming proficient with theses language patterns and the power words & phrases accomplishes several things:

- Creates depth and warmth in your conversations

- Makes your conversations more interesting

- Reaches directly into the subconscious mind of your listener

If I ask you, for example, "why did you come tonight?" You will give me a rationalized answer. However, if I ask you, "for what purpose did you come tonight?" the response would be much different. "Why" is cognitive, while "purpose" is subconscious. If I ask your purpose, you instantly go into your head to figure out what if any purpose you have for being there. The more "why" questions you can replace the more unconscious processes you will draw out.

Beginning questions with "In what way…" or "For what purpose…' "To what end…" etc. richens your conversation and forces the other person to reach into their subconscious for the answers, rather than getting some off the top of their head response.

Utilizing the speech patterns in conjunction with the power words and phrases becomes completely natural very quickly and takes you one step further down the path to true subconscious influence and response.

In sales we talk about assumptive selling, then go out and try to appeal to the prospects conscious mind to do so.

We say things like "when you take possession of the _____, you'll be very happy you did".

However, if we were to say something like, "What will it be like, for you, as you begin to use this _____," or "You really shouldn't buy this_____ until you've satisfied yourself that this is the right decision for you."

Or maybe something like, "When you take possession of this_____, you'll begin to notice an amazing sense of pride, knowing that you've made the right decision for you and your family. Haven't you?"

These examples demonstrate context that directly affect the subconscious mind. It works in writing, but much better verbally. However; if used judiciously, they can be extremely potent when written as well. If you look at the text of this book, you'll notice I use it quite prolifically.

That concludes the Persuasion and Influence language key of this book. We could literally spend weeks on this one subject alone. In terms of verbal communication these language patterns are vital. With no more than I've given you here you can begin to apply this information to the extent that you'll be able to see an amazing transformation begin in your interpersonal communication skills. I hope you will.

« Chapter 11 »
Gate 3, Terminal D

I recently took a trip to New York City to see a friend of mine speak at a business conference. Little did I realize what I was in for on this quick up and back trip to New York. It was simple; I would fly from Nashville to New York, attend the conference, spend the night, then fly back the next day.

Two things happened on this trip aside from getting to see my friend and attending the conference. First, I got a real lesson on doing things on the cheap. Secondly, I was reminded of a truth I'd known for years but had forgotten, or maybe ignored. When it came back to me it was like an epiphany.

I tend to over complicate things and am almost always pressed for time to get things done. This time was going to be different. I picked a hotel that was less than one block from the venue. This would save me the cost of transportation to and from the event. It was and even better because the Holiday Inn Express I chose was also the cheapest hotel in that part of Manhattan.

I planned to book a flight that would arrive early in the afternoon which would give me ample time to get from LaGuardia to my hotel, get checked in and be early to the conference. I would stay the night, then planned to have the entire next day in the city before flying back out that evening. You know what they say about the best laid plans.

Things began to go sideways before I even started for New York. The person putting on the conference oversold the venue and had to move the event nearly two miles from my hotel, which meant I would have to take a taxi to and from my hotel. That was adding expense, but the Holliday Inn Express was still the cheapest hotel in the area.

It came time to book my flight. I went on line looking for discount fares and found a company that had an American Airlines flight that appeared to be perfect. It left Nashville at around 11:00 and arrived in New York at 2:00, or so I thought.

I could choose between an economy ticket which is nontransferable, nonrefundable, I could choose the normal ticket which could be transferred or refunded, or I could fly first class. Thinking I was saving money I chose the economy ticket for $385 +/- a dollar or so. So now I'm staying at the cheapest hotel and taking the cheapest flight…or so I thought.

The night before I was to leave, I went on line to confirm my flight. I noticed something was terribly wrong. What I thought was a direct flight to New York was actually a connecting flight in Philadelphia. The layover was 19 hours! I was going to arrive in New York at 2:00 the day after the conference with a returning flight at 7:30 that evening!

I called the travel company that booked my flight and they said since it was a non-changeable ticket, they couldn't help me and recommended I call American direct. When I spoke with the airline, they told me the same thing. In order to get to New York, I had to buy a new one-way ticket for $575. I booked it all the while planning to use the second half of the first ticket to get back home.

When I arrived in New York I began looking for a taxi to the event. My new ticket didn't give me time to get to the hotel to check in beforehand, so I decided to call the Holiday Inn to confirm my reservation. I called and they had no reservation for me. They asked me where I was supposed to be staying. I told them "the Holiday Inn Express in mid-town Manhattan. To which they responded, "There are five."

I called IHG who found my reservation and gave me the confirmation number and the number of the hotel. I called the hotel they gave me. It was the same one I had called originally. When I gave them the confirmation number, they found my reservation immediately.

I couldn't believe there were no taxis. Finally, I found someone who told me where the taxi stand was, so I raced over. As I approached, this young man asked if I was needing a taxi. I, of course, said yes.

He motioned a car up to the stand and without thinking I got in and gave the address to the young lady who was driving. About half-way to Manhattan I said something to the effect that this was not what I was expecting when I asked for a taxi. The girl responded with, "Oh, this isn't a taxi; it's a private car service."

While I was happy to have a ride of any sort, I was not excited about what I knew was going to be an expensive ride. When it was all said and done, it cost me over $80 to get out of the car.

When I finally arrived at the event it was 15 minutes in to my friends 30-minute presentation. The event went very well, and I had a great time. After everything was over, I needed to get a ride to my hotel. I called the girl who drove me to the event to see if she could take me to my hotel.

Even though it was a little pricey, she was now a "known" to me, so I hoped I could stick with her for my ride. Unfortunately, her shift had ended, and I would have to give an hour's notice to get another driver (and I should have too).

I didn't figure I could hail a cab so I called a taxi service who said they would send someone to get me right away. I stood on the street in mid-town Manhattan for an hour at 11:30 at night in the freezing cold before I called back to see where my ride was. I was told they would check and call me back. The call didn't come.

After another 30 minutes I called back, only to be told that the car they'd sent had broken down and I had no ride. I had never taken an Uber or a Lyft before and was a bit reluctant but went ahead and called. In just a matter of a few minutes my ride showed up and took me to my hotel. I arrived at about 1:00 a.m.

When I got to my room, I went back online to confirm my return flight. I went on the site only to find my ticket had been cancelled. Once again, I called the airline. I was informed that because I hadn't taken the first half of my ticket, the second half had been cancelled. So, I had no choice. "How much is a one-way flight to Nashville," I asked. "$325," I was told. So, I booked the flight, which left New York at 9:00a.m. rather than the 7:30p.m. I'd planned. So, my day in the city was no more.

I arrived at my gate about 30 minutes early. At approximately the time my flight was supposed to be arriving, they announced that it was running about an hour late. I sat there for a little while, then decided to go to the restroom, get a drink and buy my wife a souvenir before boarding.

When I got back to my gate, it was empty, the jetway was locked and I looked out the window at the pilot of the jet I was supposed to be on. To this day I don't know how they could have arrived gotten everyone off, reloaded and ready to leave in that time.

I went to the agents at the adjacent gate. I said, "do you see that jet sitting out there? I'm supposed to be on it." They told me they could get me on another flight that wasn't a direct flight but would get me to Nashville. I told them I didn't care where it connected if they could just get me out of New York, and to please not tell me it was going to cost me another $350 or more to replace my nontransferable ticket.

They graciously transferred the ticket. However, my new flight was going to be leaving within the hour and was at Gate 3 in Terminal D, I was in Terminal B, no way could I make that flight. Fortunately, they allowed me to take an internal shuttle that took me across the tarmac to Terminal D, giving me plenty of time to get to Gate 3 and catch my flight.

It was sitting there in Gate 3, Terminal D that I began to reflect on everything that had happened to me on this trip. It was my fault for not double checking my first ticket. It was my fault for not confirming that I could retain the second half of that ticket. It was my fault for not being better prepared to get ground transportation at the airport. It was my fault for not confirming my hotel reservation until I arrived in New York and not having my confirmation number with me. It was my fault that I arrived 15 minutes late to my event and my fault that I missed my return flight. But I realized that my fault went much deeper than that. It was my fault for being in the position to even do what I had done.

I remembered back to my younger days as a defense contractor and what it was like to really have money. Back then I wouldn't have bought the cheapest airline ticket possible, I wouldn't have stayed in the Holiday Inn Express. I would have bought the better ticket and stayed in a nice hotel. I wouldn't have hesitated to take a private car service to get me where I needed to go. And it all came back to me.

Do you know what wealthy people do not do?

Wealthy people don't call the airline and ask when they can fly. They tell someone to prep their plane and be ready to leave at the time that's best for them not the airline.

Wealthy people don't get humiliated by going through TSA's security check where you have to take off your shoes and belt, have all your personal belongings searched, and have a nude picture taken all while being treated like a potential terrorist.

Wealthy people don't "catch" a flight. They wait for the plane to come to them while they sit comfortably in the lounge drinking coffee from a china cup.

Wealthy people don't have to stuff their self into a seat that's crammed against the person next to them, with no leg room. They sit comfortably in a leather chair where they can stretch their legs out while being served pretty much whatever they want whenever they want.

Wealthy people don't wait for the serving cart to come by at the flight attendant's convenience to offer them a soft drink and pretzels. They get served pretty much whatever they want whenever they want at their request.

Wealthy people don't chase down taxis or call uber. They have a private car service pick them up where and when they want, and the car shows up at that time, takes them where ever they want to go, then picks them up, or wait for them until they're ready to go again.

Wealthy people don't stay in discount hotels. They stay in the best hotels. Not because they're expensive, but because they know their needs will be met without hesitation. They know that there is no potential for networking opportunities at the Holiday Inn Express. People with money are not there. The networking opportunities are at the nice hotels, the four-star hotels.

But there I sat in Gate 3 Terminal D, frustrated, exhausted and angry. Not with the airline, or the hotel, but with myself. How did I let myself get to this point? Why was I allowing myself to be in this position?

Then it dawned on me. I had become, in the words of Pink Floyd, "comfortably numb". In that song it says,

> ***"when I was a child, I caught a fleeting glimpse, out of the corner of my eye. I turned to look but it was gone. I cannot put my finger on it now. The child has grown, the dream has gone. I have become comfortably numb."***

I had been beaten down so many times that I had become numb to my situation. I had settled for the minimum. I was no longer the "overcomer" I once was. I had become a "settler". I had lost that child-like ability to dream, where nothing was impossible. I was no longer that hair on fire risk taker I used to be. I had become comfortable with being "safe". There is no more dangerous, no riskier place you can be than "safe". Being safe drains you of your strength, your vision and your ability to succeed. There is no place for hopes and dreams when you're being safe.

Sure, I was pretending to be an entrepreneur, someone important, when in reality I had become no more than a common thief. By settling, by becoming comfortably numb, I was stealing from my wife, my children, my parents, potential employees and clients that should have been benefiting from what I have to offer.

It was there, in Gate 3 Terminal D that I drew a line in the sand. No longer would I do everything on the cheap. No longer would I settle for not having the tools I need for my business.

No longer would I settle for anything less than I am capable of and what I deserve. I have no excuse for staying in the "Safe Zone," where there is no hope now. I had to become what I once was again.

It was there, in Gate 3 Terminal D, that I became alive again. I was no longer comfortably numb. I determined at that moment that things would change.

How many people do you know, maybe someone very "close" to you who had become comfortably numb? You see, being comfortably numb is not about money. You can be making a seven-figure income and still be comfortably numb. Being comfortably numb is about complacency.

It's about settling for less than you are capable of because you believe it's not risky to remain who you are, where you are and you couldn't be more wrong. It's scary to step outside your comfort zone in order to become more.

The popular belief today is that we need to learn that we are "enough", just as we are. As a human being that may be true, but as a person we should never be "enough." Because when you're enough, you quit growing, you quit learning, you quit becoming more than enough.

How many times do we make our decisions based on the price rather than the cost? When we shop on price, we almost always increase our cost. Which is the least expensive, a stay at an economy hotel or a luxury hotel? If you're not interested in meeting people at a level above yours, you would pick the economy hotel. If, however, you're looking to grow and evolve yourself and your business, the economy hotel is far more expensive.

Which is cheaper, stuffing yourself in an economy seat on an airline, or flying comfortably in first class? The same applies. You will most likely not meet anyone who will advance your brand and your business in the economy seats. The people who can help your business and help you grow your brand are in first class, which means the $385 economy ticket is far more expensive than the $950 first class ticket.

You see, so many of us are so focused on the "price" of things that we never calculate the "cost".

When I ran the numbers on my trip to New York, I found something amazing. For what I had spent trying to do everything on the cheap, all the frustration of not paying for precheck, dealing with the cramped seat, the tiny hotel room and trying to find transportation I didn't save any money at all.

In fact, for what I paid to do things on the cheap, I could have flown first class round trip, stayed in a four-star hotel, and had a private car service take me everywhere I wanted to go! Not to mention, the only time I was around anyone who could advance my brand and my business was the five hours I was in the business conference, rather than the twenty plus hours I spent outside the conference.

Was it cheaper for me to avoid paying doctors for annual checkups for 20 years, eat cheap unhealthy foods and avoid going to the gym or to spend the time and money to take care of myself?

When I was finally forced to go to the doctor I was dying, and the weight of the medical bills destroyed me financially. It would have been far less expensive in both dollars and my health to have taken the necessary steps to take care of myself before it was nearly too late to do so.

When you make purchases for your business, are you making your decisions based on price or cost? Do you buy the cheapest computer with barely enough power to do what you need today, rather than one that will comfortably operate your business for two years?

I once worked for a company whose owner listened to the controller's advice and decided to make everyone save their used paper to be cut up and repurposed as "scratch paper" so the company could save a few dollars on note pads.

Do you know what a twenty-million-dollar company saves reusing printer paper? The answer is nothing. In fact, it cost them money. By the time you consider the cost of labor, the low quality, and the morale lowering affect it has on the team members, it cost that company a fortune.

You are capable of more than you are currently doing. You're capable of more physically, spiritually and financially. Do what you're worthy of. You are worthy of so much more than you currently have. Take charge, take control, and don't settle. Put yourself out there. Take a chance on the one sure thing you can invest in. Investing in you and your team is the best most profitable investment you can make.

It doesn't have to be complicated. If you're working forty-hour weeks increase it to sixty. If you do, you'll work the equivalent of three years every two. Do you think, even if you're on salary, that increasing your production by 33% would increase your income? There's no doubt about it.

I would challenge you. Don't wait until your body, your finances and your relationships are beyond saving. Don't wait for a Gate 3 Terminal D to realize you are worthy of more. If yourself having become comfortably numb it's not too late. Change! And do it now.

« Summary »

To wrap up this book, I would like to thank you for staying with me for the duration. As you've seen and heard, "The Mind Hackers Guide to Selling" is a comprehensive training & coaching system designed to help sales and other professionals take their interpersonal communication skills to a new level. This new level will empower you/them to quickly and automatically be more persuasive, more powerful and ultimately more profitable.

Sales professionals, who have been trained in just one of the five keys covered here, will, on average increase their business by 20% or more. Even if the increase were half that or even half of that, it would still be an annual increase of 5% on top of any increases they would otherwise achieve. A 5-20% annual increase when considering the law of compounding is an amazing return on investment.

Even if I were to charge your company the full price for my training including the monthly coaching I offer, the return would still be much more than the investment. Imagine investing in something that has a potential 100% first year ROI! If the cost is zero, it is difficult to justify not having me train and coach your sales team, your management staff and anyone else you choose.

As you go back through this information again, you'll have an even better idea as to the powerful benefits "The Mind Hackers Guide to Selling" can offer your company.

"The Mind Hackers Guide to Selling" is unlike any other training & coaching program in the world as far as I know. There are professionals who teach each of the five keys independently but none who train all five comprehensively. Additionally, most of those professional trainers are just that, professional trainers. Most have no practical sales and management experience spanning over 30+ years as I do.

This means, they are trying to fit selling into their science. We on the other hand take the opposite approach. We fit the science into selling and that means you will not have to alter your processes in order to make the system work.

"The Mind Hackers Guide to Selling" is designed with sales in mind.

As you begin this training you will notice for yourself that it's not something separate from what you've been trained or what you currently use, but rather you will find it to be a perfect companion to your existing sales process. And what's particularly powerful about this system is that your team will love it.

Even though "The Mind Hackers Guide to Selling" is based on advanced neuro-psychology and psycho-physiology your team will find it very easy to learn and implement. Each key is designed so it will immediately enhance your team's communication skills in a way that feels natural.

You'll also find that your team is more compelling, more confident and more comfortable offering your solutions to their prospects and clients. They will have the skills to more effectively demonstrate why and how your solution is the best solution for the prospect in a way that feels good to them. Your team will be able to instinctively communicate with others in precisely the way they naturally process information and thought.

I hope you've enjoyed this book and look forward to establishing a long-term relationship that is profitable for you, your clients and even for me.

For booking information to have me present a Keynote speech, a breakout presentation, executive brief, training and/or coaching you can reach me at:

615-388-1389

By email at james@allncom.com

You can follow me on:
Facebook @ allncom

Twitter @James_G_Springer

Or LinkedIn @jamesgspringer

www.ingramcontent.com/pod-product-compliance
Lightning Source LLC
Chambersburg PA
CBHW021440210526
45463CB00002B/593